THE GI BILL

THE GI BILL
The Law That Changed America

Milton Greenberg

Lickle Publishing Inc

Published by Lickle Publishing Inc
590 Madison Avenue
New York, NY 10022

Library of Congress Catalog Card Number: 97-69957

Printed in the United States

American Legion
D.C. Public Library
Library of Congress
National Archives
The New York Public Library
Veterans Administration

American Council on Education
Indiana University
Marietta College
University of Maryland
University of Wisconsin-Extension
Wayne State University

Don A. Balfour
Harry Belafonte
Michael Bennett
Ruth Bragg
Andrew Brimmer
Art Buchwald
Phil Budahn
Dorothy Chamberlain
Senator Bob Dole
Gail Donovan
Irv Feinman
Sonia Greenberg
Karl Heymann
Stanley Kosierowski
Arnold A. Lear
Leon Lederman
Sophia Maroon
George Merritt
Willis Messiah
Lewis Milford
William Norris
Joan Munkasci
Susan O'Connell
Kay O'Grady
Keith Olsen
Dovey Roundtree
Karen Thomas
June Willenz
Reginald Wilson

Ladies Home Journal

Contents

Foreword

by Senator Bob Dole

Before the end of the war, the mood of our country was very good. The United States made a great contribution by defending a community of values unique to all the world. During this period, our economy was prospering and unemployment was low. It was a very exciting time.

But when we came home, things were different. What would our country do with millions of returning veterans? Thanks to the GI Bill of Rights, individuals were given many different opportunities and equipped with many different skills. Were it not for this program, veterans might have found themselves unemployed, standing in a bread line. We had a government that knew its proper role as a neighbor not a warden—a government that was lending a helping hand. I think the GI Bill paid off many, many times what it cost.

Many of our country's young people had just graduated from high school or were still in college when they were called to serve. Some were skilled but many were working for a living during the war, and for millions of veterans in the service it was a step up. In my case,

I went from a couple of nondescript years in college before the war, and came back and made excellent grades. I went on to law school and got involved in politics. None of that would have happened without the GI Bill and I am certain that everybody had a different story.

In addition to all these veterans getting an education, they understood how important education was for their children. So it had an impact on future generations. If your father went to college, he would want you to go to college.

It didn't make any difference what my parent's income was or the fact that my dad wore his overalls everyday to work. I still got the benefit and I think that is something that was there for everybody. No discrimination, no special privileges for anyone.

You look at what happened with all these young men and women who then went on to succeed in every different field—they went into politics, they became actors, they were in the Federal Reserve. They were productive citizens—small business men and women and homeowners.

The GI Bill changed America, it may have changed the world.

Introduction

THE LAW THAT CHANGED AMERICA

The Servicemen's Readjustment Act of 1944, brilliantly dubbed "The GI Bill of Rights" by the American Legion, was one of the most important, successful, lasting, and, in retrospect, almost romantic contributions to American history. The law made available to sixteen million veterans of World War II immediate financial support of unemployment insurance, generous educational opportunities ranging from vocational job training to higher education, and home ownership. This combination of opportunities changed the social and economic landscape of America. It was the American Dream come true.

The war in Europe was won in May, 1945 after a prolonged march through many nations, cities, and streets, and the greatest amphibious invasion ever staged. The Pacific war, a deadly naval and island hopping contest, ended rather abruptly in August after the dropping of the Atomic Bomb on Japan. Demobilization faced the nation.

Because of the Depression years through which most veterans had grown up, few had a high school education, most had never worked, few had lived in family-owned homes. The future was uncertain but each had a major "ace in the hole"—the GI Bill of Rights.

PLANNING FOR THE RETURN

Franklin Delano Roosevelt in a July 1943 radio "fireside chat" to the nation. "Veterans must not be demobilized into an environment of inflation and unemployment, to a place on a bread line or on a corner selling apples. We must this time have plans ready."

THE AMERICAN LEGION

As early as 1942, President Roosevelt initiated planning for demobilization, acutely aware of the inevitable issues looming whenever the war ended. In fall 1942 he submitted some proposals to Congress, including furlough pay, medical care, and limited education and training programs.

In July 1943, with the tide of the war turning more clearly favorable to the Allies, President Roosevelt spoke to the nation. "Veterans must not be demobilized into an environment of inflation and unemployment, to a place on a bread line or on a corner selling apples. We must this time have plans ready." Congressman Hamilton Fish of New York clearly expressed the underlying fear, warning that veterans must not "come home and sell apples as they did after the last war, because if that is all they were offered, I believe we would have chaotic and revolutionary conditions in America." The 1920s and 1930s produced much evidence of the rise of totalitarian dictatorships of the left and right in many nations, especially in Germany, a formerly democratic and highly developed society.

Hundreds of legislative proposals were placed before Congress but none captured the public imagination or strong political support.

Enter the American Legion. Founded in 1919 as a veterans advocacy

President Franklin Delano Roosevelt signing the GI Bill June 22, 1944.

group, the Legion, held its twenty-fifth annual convention in September, 1943. The Legion initiated its own campaign for comprehensive support of veterans and named a special committee which met for about two weeks over Christmas in Washington, D.C.'s Mayflower Hotel.

Credited with being the architect of the Legion proposal is Harry W. Colmery, of Kansas, an attorney, a World War I veteran and former national commander of the Legion. In a legendary effort, he drafted the essence of the law on the back of hotel stationery in Room 507 of the Mayflower Hotel. He could not have foreseen the revolution in American culture he had wrought. The Legion called their proposal "a bill of rights for GI Joe and GI Jane." The press and history dubbed it the GI Bill of Rights. Imagine: the right to an education, employment services, a loan for a home of your own.

The term GI is an abbreviation for "Government Issue" which refers to the standardization of military regulations or equipment (GI boots, for example). But it came to signify an enlisted man in any branch of service. Adding "bill of rights" to the term combined two enormously powerful images.

The bill was introduced in Congress on January 10, 1944. President Roosevelt signed it on June 22: The Servicemen's Readjustment Act of 1944.

The story of the passage of the bill into law falls into the "truth is stranger than fiction" file. President Roosevelt feared that the Legion proposal would interfere with the proposals he had before Congress. Many educators opposed it as a threat to higher education standards. Other veterans organizations dedicated to disabled veterans feared that funds would be diverted from the most needy. Unions enjoying the protection of closed shops were cautious, and bankers feared government involvement in loans. And, racial discrimination, legally commonplace at that time, including segregated military forces, became an issue regarding opportunities for black veterans.

The five months between introduction and passage were filled with drama. The campaign by the American Legion was a model for its time, using radio spots narrated by wounded veterans, short film clips in theaters, mail, petitions, and direct pressure on members of Congress by every Legion post. A major radio address by the national commander of the Legion, Warren H. Atherton, warned that the returning veterans could "make our country or break it" and "restore our democracy or scrap it."

The Legion had a vital ally—William Randolph Hearst who controlled a major chain of newspapers. Hearst had opposed America's entry into the war but he made passage of the Legion proposal a personal campaign. Author Joseph Goulden summed it up: "He was the most powerful press man in America. And when William Randolph Hearst snapped his fingers, things happened around the country. He made this a full court press issue." Goulden points out that in a time without television the strong support of a newspaper was something to be taken seriously.

THE TERM GI IS AN ABBREVIATION FOR "GOVERNMENT ISSUE" WHICH REFERS TO THE STANDARDIZATION OF MILITARY REGULATIONS OR EQUIPMENT (GI BOOTS, FOR EXAMPLE). BUT IT CAME TO SIGNIFY AN ENLISTED PERSON IN ANY BRANCH OF SERVICE. ADDING "BILL OF RIGHTS" TO THE TERM COMBINED TWO ENORMOUSLY POWERFUL IMAGES.

Harry W. Colmery.

Mayflower Hotel.

Harry W. Colmery's legendary handwritten draft of the GI Bill and early Senate versions of the law that changed America.

Warren H. Atherton. He warned the nation of the need to consider the future of returning veterans.

The "war room" of American Legion Legislative Director Francis M. Sullivan with piles of petitions and letters in support of the GI Bill then pending in Congress.

Twelve of the "first team" that quarterbacked the creation and passage of the first GI Bill. Front row, left to right: Lyon W. Brandon (Mississippi); Roane Waring (Tennessee); Rep. John Gibson (Georgia); Harry W. Colmery (Kansas); Pat Kelley (Georgia.); Frank Reilly (Massachusetts).
Back row: Frank Sullivan (Washington D.C.); John Stelle (Illinois); David Camelon (New York); Sam Rorex (Arkansas); Jack Cejnar (Indiana) and T. O. Kraabel (North Dakota.)
    No photo ever was ever taken of the whole group. Of those shown. Stelle was chairman of the Legion's original GI Bill committee, while Colmery and Rorex were members. Camelon and Reilly were assigned by Hearst newspapers to help. Sullivan, Kraabel and Cejnar were key Legion staff members in the drive. Rep. Gibson made the "midnight ride" from Georgia to cast the deciding vote that saved the bill from defeat in Congress. Waring and Kelley helped get him there.

THE GI BILL IS ENACTED

In Congress the bill had strong support and passed both houses but in slightly different versions. A conference committee called to resolve differences was chaired by Representative John Rankin, an open racist from Mississippi, who strongly opposed the New Deal. He objected specifically to that portion of the bill which provided unemployment insurance to veterans (the 52-20 Club) because it would afford blacks the same compensation as whites.

The committee deadlocked but only because Rankin refused to cast the vote of Representative John Gibson of Georgia whose proxy for passage he held. Gibson could not be found and a decisive vote was scheduled for the next day, June 10, at 10:00 A.M

With the help of the American Legion, the Hearst press, radio stations, police, and telephone operators, Gibson was finally tracked down. A wild car ride followed by a specially arranged flight to Washington brought Gibson to the conference on time. It was just four days after the June 6, D-Day landing at Normandy Beach. Men are dying in Normandy, Gibson reminded his colleagues.

The Servicemen's Readjustment Act of 1944 was signed by President Roosevelt on June 22, 1944 with five American Legion members, including Harry Colmery, looking on. On the fiftieth anniversary of that day, June 22, 1994, President William J. Clinton said that the legacy of the GI Bill of Rights was the world's largest middle class and the world's strongest economy.

Four elements of the GI Bill were revolutionary as post-war benefits for all veterans:

- readjustment allowances while unemployed
- educational opportunity in colleges and universities
- vocational education and on-the-job training
- loans for purchase of a home, farm, or business

Other provisions aided veterans to find jobs, provided for medical benefits and hospitalization, and even called for a review of military discharges other than honorable so as to avoid possible injustices.

The nation's attention was fixed on the historical drama unfolding in Europe after D-Day and only modest notice was given to passage of the GI Bill except by the Hearst press. Few people, including many closely connected to its development, were aware of the implications of the law. Commentary of that time tended to stress the costs of the 52-20 club and mention the education and loan programs as "other" parts of the law. In fact, few servicemen then in uniform or the general public were even aware of the bill, much less its consequence. A study by the Army in 1944 of enlisted men stationed in the United States

Representative John Rankin of Mississippi almost killed the GI Bill.

JOHN GIBSON

'44 Model Paul Revere Rides to Washington to Save Rights Bill

Daring Dash from Southern Georgia, Through Rain and Darkness, Saves Legislation

All the elements of a motion picture play — drama, suspense, a wild drive across country at night through a driving rain, an airplane flight, and the surprise finish that made right and justice triumphant — were part of the closing sessions of the joint Senate-House conference committee when a compromise on The American Legion's Bill of Rights for War II veterans, acceptable to both houses, was agreed upon.

The leading character was Representative John S. Gibson, member of the lower House from Georgia's Eighth District. He was the 1944 model Paul Revere who rode through the night, braving dangers that the 1775 Paul could not dream

REP. JOHN S. GIBSON

Representative John Gibson of Georgia completes his "midnight ride" to rescue the GI Bill.

REP. GIBSON GETS THERE ON TIME

DASH FOR THE CAPITAL

Finds Clear-Sailing for the "GI Bill of Rights"

Flying Gibson Casts GI Compromise Ballot

Georgian in Mad Rush To Save 'GI' Measure

A mad race against time over the highways of south Georgia, then through the air in an Eastern Air Lines plane from Jacksonville to Washington, is being staged this morning in an effort to get Congressman John S. Gibson, of the eighth Georgia congressional district, back in Washington in time to break a deadlock on the "GI Bill of Rights" bill.

3-Week Deadlock On GI Bill Smashed; All Benefits Kept

Gibson's Dramatic Race Despite Illness Puts Measure Over

showed that few knew of the bill's existence. To this day, few WW II veterans recall where, when or how they first heard of the GI Bill.

Within weeks, each of the major elements of the GI Bill took on life and title of its own. The unemployment compensation plan was dubbed the "52-20 Club" for $20 per week for up to a year. Training programs were vocational in nature and often managed by employers to train their own workers. It was the higher education portion that became synonymous with the term "GI Bill" and which evokes the most emotion. The loan provisions became known as "VA loans" referring to the Veterans Administration's supervision.

Veterans still say:"The 52-20 Club sure helped for a short while," until "I went to college on the GI Bill," and then "I took out a VA loan to buy my first house."

THE 52-20 CLUB

The portion of the GI Bill which almost killed it before passage became the centerpiece of the legislation for most GIs upon discharge from service. It authorized a "readjustment allowance" of $20 per week for up to fifty-two weeks while a veteran sought employment. Fear of massive unemployment dominated the minds of that generation and easy access to the weekly stipend was a calming influence.

For many veterans, it provided a necessary "cool down" period. Although World War II is remembered almost fondly, the brutality and fear of combat was experienced by millions. Military life had occupied their maturing years. Able-bodied veterans of that war were not generally accorded the sympathy for, or understanding of post-traumatic stress which has characterized treatment of combat veterans since that time. Many veterans had a difficult time simply returning to the less disciplined civilian life and to family and friends from whom they had a lengthy separation.

Many veterans recall with nostalgia that $20 was a lot of money in the mid-1940s. For fifteen cents or less you could buy gasoline, cigarettes, beer, milk shakes, go to a movie. Some veterans refused to apply for the $20 per week, looking upon it with disdain as a form of welfare. Skeptics about the GI Bill called it a giveaway that would lead to irresponsible idleness. Contrary to that expectation, from 1944 to 1949, about nine million of sixteen million eligible veterans "joined the club" but on average, used it for only seventeen weeks before finding a job or going to school. An average of four months time to get back in gear seems reasonable. Less than twenty percent of the estimated cost of the program was actually spent.

EACH ELEMENT OF THE GI BILL TOOK ON LIFE OF IT'S OWN. VETERANS STILL SAY: "THE 52-20 CLUB SURE HELPED FOR A SHORT WHILE" UNTIL "I WENT TO COLLEGE ON THE GI BILL." AND THEN "I TOOK OUT A VA LOAN TO BUY MY FIRST HOUSE."

COLLIER'S

WILLIAM L. CHENERY — Publisher

WALTER DAVENPORT — Editor

JOE ALEX MORRIS — Managing Editor

52-20 AND BUST

THE Veterans Administration is no little worried over the repeater phase of the 52-20 Club. A considerable percentage of veterans have got jobs, have quit drawing their $20 a week jobless insurance pay, and then have dropped the jobs and gone back to the 52-20 Club —so called because a veteran is entitled to 52 weeks' payments of $20 each while out of work.

Up to last July 1st, about 7,100,000 claims for these payments had been filed. Of that number, about 1,500,000 were repeater claims.

Most of these men presumably felt that it would be pleasanter to draw $20 a week for loafing than to work 40 hours a week for $25 or $30 minus Social Security taxes.

We can't sympathize with that attitude; but that attitude exists. Is there anything that can be done about it? We have a labor shortage in this country now, with numerous jobs begging to be filled.

How would it be to let the 52-20 boys remain in the club even after they take low-paid jobs? The top limit might be put at $45 a week—meaning that a man would go on drawing the $20 from the government till his job took to paying $45 or more.

Such a revision of the present system ought to furnish an incentive to many of the boys to go out and get to work and quit loafing. It would be vulnerable to abuses and chiseling, true, on the part of both some veterans and some employers. But the chiseling could be continuously combated by the Veterans Administration, and meanwhile we'd get some of the work done that needs to be done.

How about serious consideration for this plan?

Remarkably few GIs abused the 52-20 Club. Nearly half didn't take it at all and only 20 percent of available funds were used.

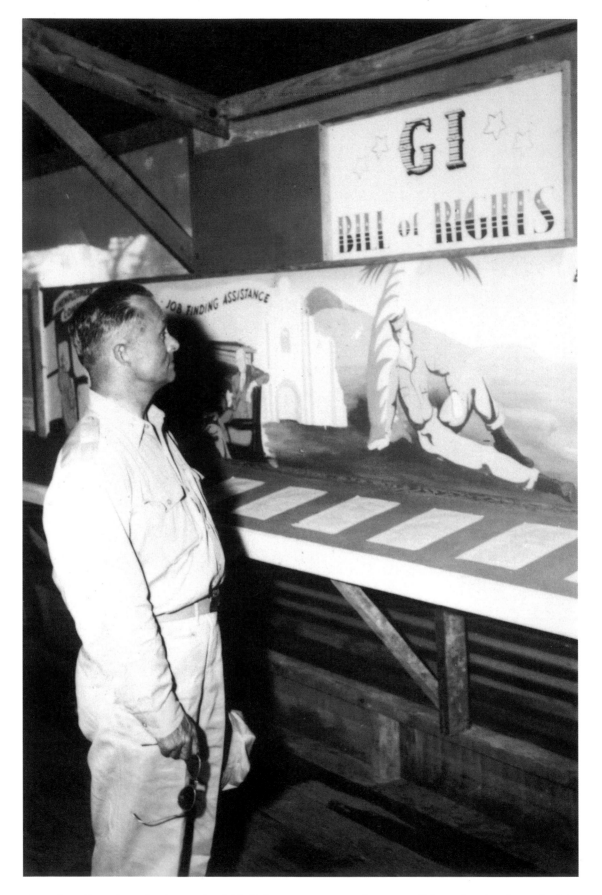

An early military base display on the GI Bill, but most veterans do not recall how they first learned of the GI Bill.

"*Son, there's a great future in aviation*"

"YES, DAD. But it seems more like just another dream now. I gave up thinking about flying when the war was over."

"I don't know why. . . . This article says that there's a big career ahead for young fellows like you in one of the biggest fields of the future . . . Aviation. It's all about the post-war Army Air Forces, and the opportunities they offer young men. Pretty interesting."

"What kind of opportunities, Dad?"

"Well, they need more technicians in the new peacetime Regular Army Air Forces than ever before. I certainly wish that I'd had half this chance when I was your age."

"What chance? How do you mean?"

"Sixty-five per cent of the men in the new Air Forces are going to be non-coms with the rank of corporal or better. That's because the new fields of aviation like jet propulsion, radar, television and radio are so complicated that you need skilled technicians to handle them. Getting to be a specialist in one of those fields would prepare a man for a big future

in civilian life. Since you've been wondering what you were going to do when you graduate from high school, I'd say that the Army Air Forces is just what you want."

"You mean enlist when I graduate and then go to college when my enlistment runs out?"

"Certainly. You can enlist for 1½, 2 or 3 year periods. The 3-year enlistment allows you to choose your branch of service. You could then go to any one of the many Army Air Forces technical schools. They're just about the best aviation schools in the world, you know! You'll learn a good trade, put it to practical use and prepare yourself for the future. When you get out, the Government will send you to college. That's part of your GI Bill of Rights."

"Gee, Dad, is that right—college free?"

"You bet! You can choose any college or university, business or trade school. After a 3-year enlistment you can have 48 months of education—a full college course—with your tuition paid up to $500 for each ordinary school year, and $65 a month living allowance—$90 if you're married."

"Guess my dreaming is going to pay off. Think I'll go down to the recruiting station in the morning!"

SEE THE JOB THROUGH

U. S. Army
BE A
"GUARDIAN OF VICTORY"

PAY PER MONTH — ENLISTED MEN	Starting Base Pay Per Month	MONTHLY RETIREMENT INCOME AFTER:	
In Addition to Food, Lodging, Clothes and Medical Care		20 Years' Service	30 Years' Service
Master Sergeant or First Sergeant	$138.00	$89.70	$155.25
Technical Sergeant	114.00	74.10	128.25
Staff Sergeant	96.00	62.40	108.00
Sergeant	78.00	50.70	87.75
Corporal	66.00	42.90	74.25
Private First Class	54.00	35.10	60.75
Private	50.00	32.50	56.25

(a)—Plus 20% Increase for Service Overseas. (b)—Plus 50% if Member of Flying Crews. (c)—Plus 5% Increase in Pay for Each 3 Years of Service.

★ **ENLIST NOW!** ★

Where would you like to go during the next three years?

France? Germany? Philippines? Japan? China? Hawaii? Panama? Puerto Rico? Alaska?

GI's in Germany

IF YOU are a red-blooded American — alert, alive and ambitious — you probably want these things: Adventure! . . . Travel to foreign lands! . . . Good pay, good food, good clothing! . . . Training for future success! . . . A thorough education!

The new peacetime Regular Army offers you *all* these things. By enlisting for 3 years you can choose your arm or branch of service and overseas theater. You may travel abroad, in Germany, Japan or other occupied areas. And you can learn a skill or trade that will enable you to earn a good living all your life.

For all this training and travel, food, clothing, quarters, dental and medical care, you pay *not one cent!*

Instead *you get good pay* with liberal furloughs and the opportunity to complete your education after discharge! Under the GI Bill of Rights, following a 3-year enlistment you are entitled to 48 months of education in the college, business or trade school you select, with tuition and incidentals paid, up to $500 per ordinary school year, and $65 a month for personal expenses if single, $90 a month if married!

Act now! Get full details at your nearest Army Recruiting Station!

SEE THE JOB THROUGH

U. S. Army
BE A
"GUARDIAN OF VICTORY"

Enlist NOW!

Army recruitment ads in 1946 using GI Bill as an incentive to encourage replacements for demobilized veterans.

Norman Rockwell asks:
"Would a Veteran find <u>You</u> here?"

The no-nonsense type. "You've been home a whole week, son. Isn't it time to look for a job? Can't pamper ourselves, you know."

The Tsk-Tsk Sister. Just can't take her eyes off a disabled soldier. Thinks it's awful, and what's more, lets him know it.

Motor Martyr. Okinawa may have been tough all right, but wait'll you hear this civilian on the rigors of rationed driving.

Americans, first-class. "Welcome home, soldier!" *Here's* where a veteran would probably find *you*, glad to see him and eager to help. Because the great majority of Americans are too grateful to these veterans to make the mistakes shown here.

Good Americans don't prod the veteran with questions if he doesn't want to talk. They don't act sorry for him. Nor tell him life has been hard here. (He's been where it *is* hard.) And they don't stare at any disability he may have.

Above all, they remember that his experiences have made him an even more resourceful, capable citizen. They make it their job to help him get back into normal civilian life. Let's *all* be like them!

Lady with the needle nose. "Tell me how it feels to be wounded, Ensign. Did you bleed much?"

Prepared by the War Advertising Council, Inc., in Cooperation with the Office of War Information and the Retraining and Reemployment Administration.

PUBLISHED IN COOPERATION WITH THE DRUG, COSMETIC AND ALLIED INDUSTRIES BY

The Reception Committee—
(KNOW ANYBODY HERE?)

The Greeter. He's a one-man brass band when it comes to welcoming a veteran. "Nothing's too good for Our Boys!" he always says. And that's exactly what he gives them. Nothing, except a big hello and empty words. Help? That's the Government's job. "Don't vets have bonuses?" he asks, "Pensions? Job agencies?"

The Bloodhound. "It's OK, Sailor, you won't shock *me!*" This shock-proof stalwart is after the details. How does it feel to be bombed? Ever knife a Jap? The War's just one big adventure to him. But it hasn't been for the sailor. He wants to forget it — *fast.* Not *talk* about it.

The Patriot. He's practically winning the war single-handed. Always talking about all the things he goes without. Mentions the War Bonds he buys as though he were doing the *Government* a favor. This makes veterans (who've been buying plenty of Bonds themselves) wonder whether we had the right people in foxholes.

The Rock. He's nerveless. The Iron Man. War hasn't affected *him.* Can't understand why discharged veterans are allowed 90 days to relax before going back to their old jobs. Can't understand why they should need time to get over the War. *He* doesn't.

Blue Ribbon Citizen. Like all good people, she asks no questions, weeps no tears, doesn't stare at disabilities. To her, a returned veteran is an abler, more aggressive and resourceful citizen than the boy who went away. She's proud of him, proud to know him. Anxious to be of real help to him. She's the kind of person we should all be.

Prepared by the War Advertising Council, Inc., in Cooperation with the Office of War Information and the Retraining and Reemployment Administration.

PUBLISHED IN COOPERATION WITH THE DRUG, COSMETIC AND ALLIED INDUSTRIES BY
LAMBERT PHARMACAL CO., St. Louis, Mo.;
Makers of **LISTERINE ANTISEPTIC**

Two advertisements from 1945 show the wide range of reaction the veterans received.

PRELUDE: WORLD WAR I AND THE GREAT DEPRESSION

ABLE BODIED VETERANS OF WORLD WAR I WERE GIVEN $60, A TRAIN TICKET HOME, AND THE PROMISE OF A $500 BONUS.

Returning veterans of World War I—"The War to end all wars."

Tanks in the nation's capital to meet the "Bonus Army"

General Douglas MacArthur (left) with aide watching the burning of a Bonus Army camp.

The Bonus March Camping Ground—after.

BELOW: *An image of the Depression years when extensive unemployment sent desperate people to soup kitchens.*

volunteers and draftees of World War II. Their parents were harsh victims of the 1930s and entire families faced a life of poverty and joblessness. Unemployment was widespread, breadlines and soup kitchens typified the era. Most of the world was caught up in the economic calamity with disastrous political results including the rise of Adolph Hitler in a crisis ridden Germany.

The outbreak of the war in Europe in 1939 brought forth a surge in economic activity and the ensuing military draft. It was the American entry into the war, following the Japanese attack on Pearl Harbor on December 7, 1941, that put an end to the Great Depression, by taking most young men out of circulation and putting everyone else to work, including large numbers of women.

World War II is called "the last great war." By the end, nearly sixteen million men and women were in military service. In September, 1940, the first peacetime draft in American history was enacted. Many volunteered but the draft continued throughout the war as men reached the age of eighteen. About 350,000 women volunteered for the various services. Over eleven million served in the Army, four million in the Navy, 600,000 in the Marines. Over 400,000 died and more than 600,000 were wounded. The home front went to work and turned the nation into an industrial giant. The tragedy of the Great Depression was temporarily forgotten. The nation was united in its support of the Allied forces against the Axis powers.

But what would happen when nearly sixteen million men returned from military service? Was it back to the breadlines and bonus marches? This was the challenge that the nation faced.

> "OUR WAY OF LIFE WAS AT RISK, AND WE WON. AND THERE'S NOTHING LIKE WINNING TO CREATE A PERCEPTION OF THE WINNERS. . . WE WERE THE VICTORS AND THE REASON WE WERE VICTORIOUS."
>
> *Lewis Milford*

Overleaf: Pages from a Collier's article paints a realistic portrait of the problems facing veterans in the early days of demobilization.

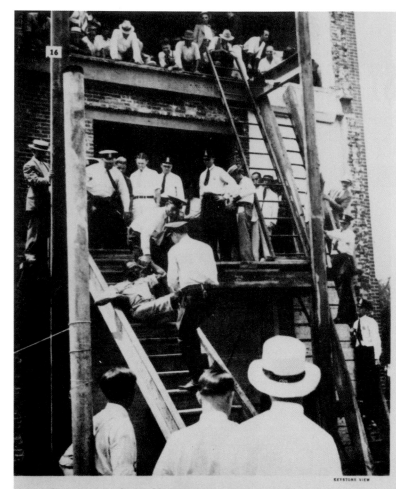

KEYSTONE VIEW

Veterans of the first world war set a precedent for concerted action with the 1932 bonus march. Here, Washington police forcibly remove them from a building

THE VETERANS SAY—*OR ELSE!*

BY AGNES E. MEYER

A distinguished journalist, in three months of travel, finds bitter disillusionment among millions of veterans. In this discontent, she says, lie the seeds of violence. Here's what our veterans are thinking—and saying

Makeshift living quarters are a prime source of veteran discontent. Below, the wives of student veterans crowd the community laundry at a Middle Western university

C. W. HUSTON-PIX

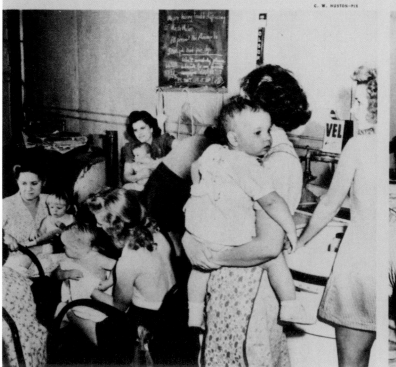

A narrow cellar room is home for these veterans and their families while they continue their education under the G.I. Bill

C. W. HUSTON-PIX

IN OUR so-called victory there is a note of despair. It comes from millions of young Americans who have returned from a brutal war. They are eager to take up life again in the homeland they did so much to save, only to find their hopes delayed and their new ideals of brotherly love thwarted by political corruption, selfishness and greed. Whether our veterans are employed or unemployed, whether they're white or black, whether they live in cities or on farms, the sum and substance of their aspirations and difficulties is the same. Their dominant mood, wherever they are, is one of dangerous cynicism and frustration.

During three months of travel, from Texas to New England, I listened with a heavy heart to what veterans have to say. I have heard them talk of jobs and housing and education, of hate and intolerance, of indifference and dishonesty. Beneath the jokes and hilarious laughter that punctuate all G.I. conversation lies a sense of appalling loneliness and bitterness.

"It is of the utmost importance that the nation should understand the nature of and the reasons for this all-prevailing mood," I was told by one of the prominent men who organized the American Veterans Committee. "The veterans are in a period of drift. Their situation contains the possibility of sudden and disastrous outbursts. Their desire for leadership is proof that a breach exists between veterans and civilians for which the homefolk are to blame."

After V-J Day the whole nation shouted: "Bring the boys home," but made no advance preparations for their return. This emotional outburst undermined our armies of occupation and crowded millions of men into an economy in which labor and capital were in a deadlock that still retards the reconversion program. Yet most people have already forgotten their first declaration that "Nothing is too good for the boys."

Such people comfort themselves with the thought that the G.I. Bill of Rights works automatically to take care of all veteran needs. Let Washington and the Veterans Administration do it, they think, complacently.

But for the veteran, it's now or never, if he is to regain the place in society he would have had if he had not gone to war. And he knows it. At present almost 2,000,000 veterans are drawing the $20 readjustment allowance, while thousands upon thousands more are applying for education and training largely because suitable employment cannot be found.

A Potential Danger

Each week, these 2,000,000 veterans receive $36,000,000. Some of these men will work out their own problems. A small number are chiselers who do not want to work. Others are not seeking employment because of emotional fatigue or dissatisfaction with the conditions that confront them. But the vast majority of these 2,000,000 unemployed veterans are floating in a vacuum of neglect, idleness and distress which is as harmful and dangerous to them as it is to the country.

We can be grateful that these men are getting their $20 weekly allowance. Except for this humane provision, we would now be experiencing bread lines, apple-selling or outright violence.

By December, however, the majority of these allowances will run out. At the same time, occupational unemployment will begin in many trades. That will be a very critical moment for the country.

In the meantime the moral, mental and economic injuries suffered by vast numbers of our soldiers are more devastating than the physical injuries of battle. The nervous breakdowns are mounting. Unless we act now, we shall multiply our later problems and run the risk of serious disorder. "You can help the veteran and prosper with him," General Omar Bradley has said, "or abandon him and pay the price of his neglect."

If you examine the "gripes" of these boys, one by one, you can understand the present dangerous state of mind in all its rational and irrational aspects.

It is impossible for comfortably established Americans to sympathize adequately with the appalling housing conditions to which the vast majority of returned veterans are subjected.

To visit almost any veteran's family, whether employed or unemployed, is to start upon an endless chain of woe. As you sit in overcrowded rooms, both wife and husband refer you to other relatives who are enduring similar or worse conditions.

"I hope all those seeking a place to live aren't going through my woes," said Raynard G., of Chicago. "I had almost five years' service including the whole European campaign and was awarded two personal citations, five battle stars, and the combat infantryman badge.

"After that I returned to my wife and two-year-old son. Sounds swell, don't it? But we have no place to live. The Mrs. lives at her mother's and her ma and I don't get along nohow. Last night we really had a go-around. She says we got to get out. Well, where do I go? I suffered a nervous state overseas, but it's nothing to what I'm going through now. I thought the Bulge was bad, but this is another Bulge. I hope all vets don't experience my battles. No V-E Day, no V-J Day for this soldier."

Robert L., also of Chicago, Illinois, tells me: "I served three years carrying high-octane gasoline on tankers in the South Pacific. Since I came home my wife and four-year-old daughter have 'visited' from one in-law to the other. There doesn't seem to be room for us anywhere and we are running out of relatives. At present we are visiting my wife's family.

Another Home is Broken

"This arrangement is dying a slow but sure death. As a last resort we have decided to board our daughter out, and my wife and I will take a sleeping room as soon as we can find one."

The real-estate dealers take a beating from these veterans because a minority of dealers have been responsible for repeated cases of bribery and injustice.

"I've been living a life separated from my wife and daughter," said Michael J. P., of Lansing, Illinois. "I've been in the service five years, not a blemish on my record, thirty months overseas. I have lived with my family seven weeks in all. Do you call it right? I've been all over. These real-estate men are not the same Americans I used to know. The war is over and I get involved in this civilian greed. Let depression come or inflation. I can face it with my family, but I can't do it this way."

And so on, endlessly. Sixty-four per cent of married veterans, 80 per

(Continued on page 115)

At Athens, Tennessee, veteran dissatisfaction flared into open rioting as ex-soldiers battled deputy sheriffs to insure an honest election. Cars in photo below were overturned in fighting

PRESS ASSOCIATION, INC.

Real hero of the ex-G.I. is General Omar N. Bradley, director of the Veterans Administration

IKE VERN-PIX

GI JOE AND GI JANE
GO TO COLLEGE

No one forecast the amazing success of the higher education opportunity afforded by the GI Bill. Most predictions, including that of President Roosevelt, estimated that college enrollments would increase by only 150,000 per year, with an eventual grand total of about 600,000 or 700,000 by the time the law expired in 1956. These were reasonable estimates in light of past experience.

> "THE GI BILL CHANGED THE LIVES OF MILLIONS BY REPLACING OLD ROADBLOCKS WITH PATHS OF OPPORTUNITY. AND, IN SO DOING, IT BOOSTED AMERICA'S WORK FORCE, IT BOOSTED AMERICA'S ECONOMY, AND REALLY, IT CHANGED THE LIFE OF OUR NATION."
>
> *President George Bush*
> (June 5, 1990)

High school graduation was a rare achievement prior to World War II. Millions of members of the armed forces had not even graduated from grammar school and many young Americans did not go beyond the tenth grade.

Prior to 1940, colleges were mostly private, small, liberal arts, elitist, white, and Protestant. In 1940 about 160,000 people earned degrees.

The graduating class of 1950 numbered about 500,000, most from state universities, having pursued both liberal arts and professional degrees. Ethnically, racially, and religiously they were and reflective of the American population.

Initial interest in the educational opportunities was disappointing, and in August 1945, *The Saturday Evening Post* carried an article "GIs Reject Education." But by 1947, there were 1,164,000 veterans registering for college on the GI Bill accounting for forty-nine percent of all enrollments. Catholic, Jewish, and black veterans sat in classrooms in many institutions for the first time. Many women's colleges became coeducational. Married students, with children, went to college. Prior to the war, marriage had been cause for dismissal at many colleges and having a child while in school was unthinkable. Over time, more than 2.2 million veterans went to college, about half of whom were the first in their families to do so. About 500,000 would not have attended except for the GI Bill. Higher education had become democratized, irrevocably altered. As the twentieth century draws to a close, the descendant of GIs have made college attendance an expectation and by

Registration at Indiana University in February 1946.

the mid 1990s enrollments soared to more than fourteen million students.

The GI Bill's association with higher education fails to account for the full measure of its educational impact. Actually, close to eight million veterans received education benefits. In addition to the 2.2 million in colleges, 3.5 million attended other schools such as business schools, trade schools, art and drama schools and even high school. About 1.4 million were involved in on-the-job training programs and 690,000 in farm training.

The education benefits were extraordinarily generous. Any veteran who served for ninety days was entitled to one year of full time education plus a period equal to their time in service up to a maximum of forty-eight months. The VA paid the school for tuition, fees and books. In addition a monthly stipend was sent to the veteran.

It has been estimated that for every dollar spent on GI Bill education benefits, the nation received as much as eight dollars in income taxes but the true value is incalculable. This could be attributed then, and even more so in the 1990s, to the correlation between increased

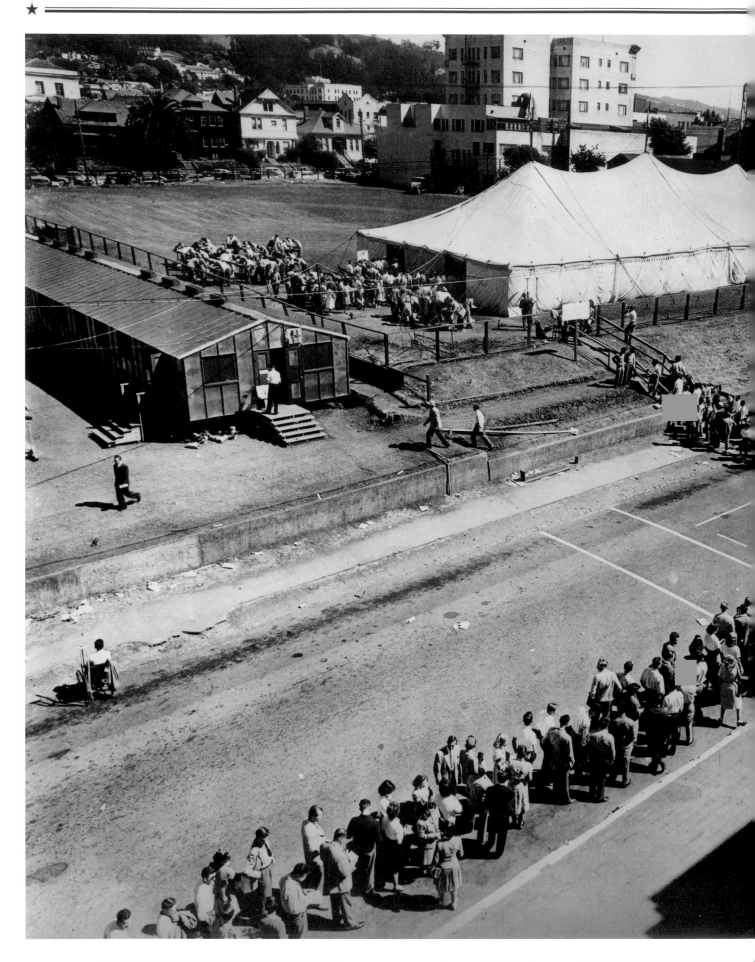

LEFT: *At the University of Denver in 1946, GIs line up to register in a scene reminiscent of army bases. Hurry up and wait!*

earning capacity and educational achievement.

It is the college and university educational provisions that endure as the symbol and romance of the GI Bill. Veterans on long lines, in crowded classrooms, living in makeshift quarters, and, in substantial numbers, married, many with children. The scene made for great newspaper, magazine, and film coverage.

Veterans applied to the college of their choice. Their eligibility was certified by the Veterans Administration and the necessary checks mailed to the school (tuition, fees, books, supplies, up to $500 per year) and to the ex-GI ($50 per month for a single veteran, $75 if married, and $15 for one or more children—amounts later raised).

The enormous success of the program was unforeseen, whether in terms of numbers attending, especially married students, the high quality of performance by veterans, or the implications of what a commitment to higher education would mean for the nation generally and higher education specifically.

Higher education associations were cautious at first and the presidents of Harvard University and The University of Chicago were outspoken in their opposition. James B. Conant of Harvard feared that unqualified people would flood the campuses. Robert M. Hutchins of Chicago, in a widely noted article in *Collier's* magazine, labeled the bill unworkable, a threat to education and warned that the lure of money would turn the colleges into "educational hobo jungles." The Hutchins article drew numerous responses and *Collier's* printed a lengthy response from Alfred E. Kuenzli who was medically discharged after two years with the Marines in the South Pacific and then enrolled at the University of Notre Dame under the GI Bill. He found the University of Chicago president's article to be "disillusioning and fallacious" and suggested that perhaps the colleges as well as the veterans required rehabilitation.

Both educational leaders had reason to eat their words eventually and Conant, in 1947 called the veterans "the most mature and promising students Harvard has ever had."

All over the nation, educators and non-veteran students were aware of the enormous achievements of veterans as competent and serious

> "THE FUNNY THING ABOUT IT, THESE SCHOLARS WERE AFRAID THAT THE GI WOULD PULL THE AVERAGE UNIVERSITY GRADES DOWN. INSTEAD OF THAT, THEY WERE THE ONES WHO MADE THE BEST GRADES."
>
> *Ernest W. McFarland*
> Former Senate Majority Leader (Arizona Republic, August 13, 1978)

Veteran students at the University of Wisconsin pose in front of familiar Quonset hut.

students. Senator, presidential candidate, and wounded veteran Robert Dole of Kansas, recalled those days when so many were in school solely because of the help of the GI Bill and said. ". . . we knew it was for real. If we were going to do anything in life, we had to settle down, go to work and study."

Most campuses took cognizance of the educational training taken by many GIs while in service. The American Council on Education, the umbrella organization for all sectors of higher education, developed a guide for evaluating military experiences so that suitable credits could be awarded, a practice continued to this day.

Educators were relieved by the easy adjustment made by most veterans to civilian student life. On many campuses, the adjustment problems were felt more by faculty who lacked experience with such mature,

OVERLEAF: *Students at Harvard, dressed in suits and ties (unlike today's style) follow registration procedure.*

LEON LEDERMAN

Lederman receiving the Nobel Prize from King Gustaf of Sweden.

Lederman at left receiving the National Medal of Science from Lyndon Johnson.

"I wanted to go to graduate school and I wanted to study physics, and while I was in Germany—the German, the European war had ended and it didn't look as if I was going to be sent to Japan or to the other war, and that was winding down, too. That's when I applied to graduate school knowing that there was the GI Bill, and that I could see surviving that way.

I also had a lot of savings because I was paid every month, and I didn't know—I never collected that money. Mostly I lived on poker winnings and, you know, meals were free, and you didn't really have any needs there.

I applied to the GI Bill. You had to be discharged before you could actually get it, but I did make applications and I applied to a number of graduate schools, but most intensely at Columbia University.

Some of the people I had met at MIT were professors at Columbia, so I pulled that, you know, don't you remember we pal'd around at MIT and I was there and so on and so on. And whether that helped or not, I don't know—but I did get accepted, and it was, in fact, helpful to—you got a quicker return home if you were accepted to a graduate school, and that was another incentive to get out of occupying Germany."

College student in 1941.

A 1947 graphic illustration of the crisis in housing on campus and in surrounding communities as over one million veterans took advantage that year of the GI Bill's educational opportunities.

knowledgeable students ("Oh, professor, I know about that. I was there"). Nonveteran male students who sought traditional college fun and access to female students, were made to appear particularly immature compared with the GIs in their khakis and flight jackets and tales of travel and war. Veterans who had lost years to war were not interested in the fun and games of fraternity life, freshmen beanies, or pep rallies.

During the peak enrollment years, veterans accounted for close to fifty percent of all enrollments and nearly seventy percent of registered male students. About 40 percent of all GI Bill students went to just thirty-eight major colleges and universities. As *TIME* magazine asked, why go to Podunk U if you can go to Yale? Many veterans preferred the professional training which larger schools could offer, leaving many smaller liberal arts colleges with unfilled space.

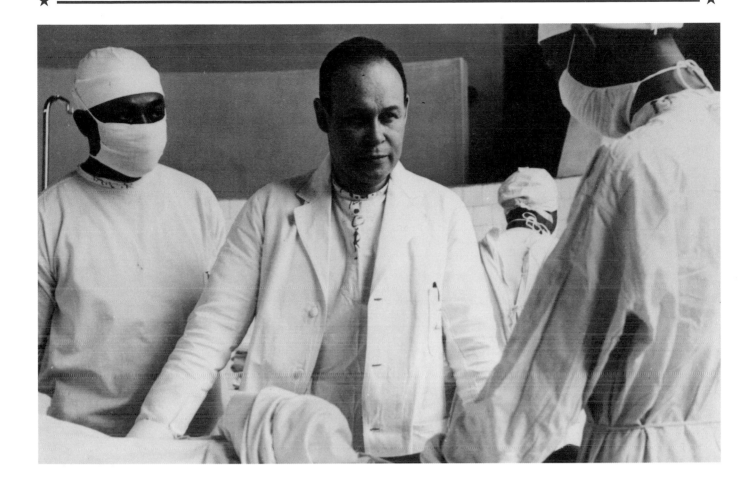

ABOVE: *Educating physicians at Howard University in Washington, D.C.*

RIGHT: *Veterans training to become veterinarians.*

They became engineers, scientists, manufacturers, doctors, dentists, accountants, lawyers, teachers and scholars. At least ten Nobel Prize winners were GIs. About fifty percent of the engineers who worked for the National Aeronautics and Space Administration (NASA) and designed or managed space flight, took their degrees under the GI Bill, most of whom would not otherwise have gone to college. Spurred by wartime applications of science and technology, college educated GIs contributed to a scientific revolution in television, computers, civil engineering, medicine, chemistry, physics, space exploration, and a continuing tradition of invention. Nobel Laureate and veteran Martin Perl put it in perspective when he commented that progress in a complex universe does not come from tinkering. What the GI Bill did was to open up opportunity "and then all these fresh minds came in and all these things were invented."

Don A. Balfour of Washington, D.C. was the first applicant for educational benefits. Balfour, who now owns an insurance agency, was a government employee and a part-time student at George Washington University after leaving the service. The day after President Roosevelt signed the GI Bill, Balfour, serving as editor of the school paper, visited the Veterans Administration to get a story about the legislation, asked if he could apply and instantly received a suitable letter. He took leave from his job which paid him $2,000 a year and instead of facing years of part-time study, accelerated his studies free of charge and received

Randall Stadium at the University of Wisconsin and adjoining "Camp Randall," a trailer park for married veterans. No running water in the trailer led to heavy use of central facilities shown in the photo to the right.

Increasingly common, but until 1945 virtually unprecedented, scenes of campus life in hastily erected, married student housing.

E. B. Fred, the President of the University of Wisconsin visits a family in "Camp Randall."

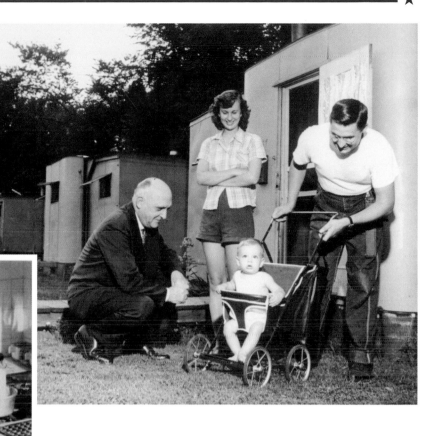

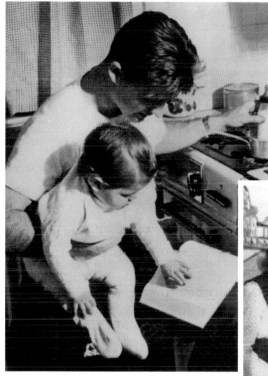

Studying under unusual circumstances.

Trailer court shopping at Indiana University.

$50 per month for expenses. "That was the best time of my life . . . I didn't have to work all day and go to school at night and then study late and not get any sleep. I could do nothing other than study and learn, and it was a great pleasure."

George Merritt, attended McAllister School of Embalming and became a licensed funeral director under the GI Bill. He lives in the legendary GI village of Levittown, New York and recalls how veterans began to accept the idea that college was not just for the rich. "I can go to school, I can get a better job, I can get an education. I can go to college, too. Not just the rich man's son."

The cover of *TIME* magazine of November 3, 1947 featured a college football star, Bob Chappius of the University of Michigan. Chappius, a radioman and gunner on a B-25 bomber was shot down over Italy, rescued by Italian partisans and hidden for several months.

The University of Michigan football team, seventy percent of whom were on the GI Bill won the Rose Bowl in 1947. Chappius was twenty-four years old at the time. He had attended the university prior to being drafted in 1942 and would likely have returned anyway. He did not win

Visiting at the trailer park at Indiana University, in this instance, foreign brides of GIs.

the Heisman Trophy in 1947, but it was won by another veteran, Johnny Lujak of Notre Dame, who had served three years as a naval officer.

GI educational benefits were available abroad as well. In 1950, the Veterans Administration reported that 5,800 veterans were studying in forty-five countries under the GI Bill. Art Buchwald, noted humorist and columnist, spent time as a GI Bill student in Paris after enrolling at the University of Southern California.

A permanent and vital legacy of the educational provisions of the GI Bill is a change in the very idea of who could be a university student. The sons of unemployed depression victims, the sons of immigrants, the children of sharecroppers were just as smart as the children of wealthy and successful industrial leaders or descendants of those who arrived on the Mayflower. Older people could share classrooms with recent high school graduates and adults could go to school while married, raising children, and working at a job.

The most often used phrase by World War II veterans who took advantage of educational opportunities remains: "I don't know where I would have been without the GI Bill."

Marietta College in Ohio anchored this surplus Coast Guard vessel in the Muskingum River to house some veterans.

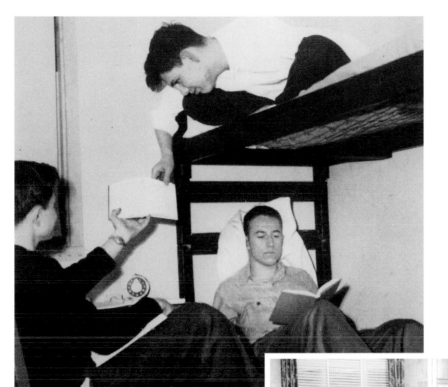

LEFT: *Studying in close quarters.*

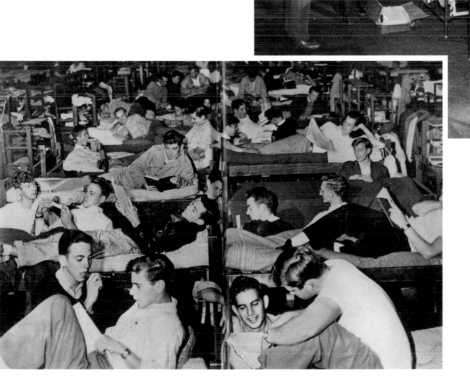

ABOVE: *The crowded situation forced students to bunk in President Herman B. Wells' board room at Indiana University.*

LEFT: *The University of Maryland houses its GI students. This extraordinary collegiate scene was replicated on campuses across the nation.*

An article from Collier's *describes the typical living situation of married GIs at college.*

CAMPUS LIVING

Few colleges and universities were prepared for the numbers of veterans who appeared to register. None were prepared for wives and children of students, a phenomenon never before experienced or even permitted.

Memories of those times unfailingly bring smiles to the faces of those who were probably not smiling then. The numbers of students on some campuses were impressive and troublesome. The University of Wisconsin grew from 9,000 to 18,000 in one year, Rutgers from 7,000 to 16,000. Registration and school cafeterias brought back memories of "hurry up and wait" in long lines. Classrooms were in short supply and were in use night and day including Saturdays. Faculty carried heavy teaching loads and text books and laboratories were not always available.

Barracks and quonset huts sprung up to house students military style. Gymnasiums and lounges were converted to lines of double decker cots. Students filled rooming houses near campus. Marietta

ANY VETERAN CAN GET A GI EDUCATION BUT THE FIRST COURSE ON HIS LIST OF SUBJECTS IS ECONOMY, WITH A CAPITAL E. AND IF HE HAPPENS TO BE MARRIED, THAT GOES DOUBLE.

DR. JERRY NAPLES

"I was twenty-five, something like that, by the time I got there [college]. I was old. And, of course, the older student who came in were the ones that really didn't fool around. I mean, we didn't get involved in fraternities and beer flings and all the rest of it. We worked, because that's what we wanted to do. That's why we were there."

Jerry Naples, valedictorian of class at Florida Southern College shown walking on the "Honor Walk" inscribed with names of outstanding students. Naples went on to medical school.

JERRY NAPLES
1950

MEET A STUDENT VETERAN

PHOTO BY MUNKACSI

Army veteran Philip Gray gets a college education at Government expense—and $109.25 monthly to support himself, wife and baby.

BY C. S. FORESTER

FOR the christening of his son Gary, ex-Corp. Philip Gray splurged the last of his Army mustering-out pay on a watermelon-red wool suit for his twenty-one-year-old wife Mary. That was fifteen months ago, and she hasn't worn it since. Not because it isn't infinitely becoming to her soft dark hair and blue eyes, but because, she explains in her soft Oklahoma drawl, she "can't hardly feature an occasion to wear it."

Cotton slacks and saddle shoes are her year-round garb as a housewife in Berkeley, California, where her twenty-three-year-old veteran husband is a student at the University of California. She rarely leaves their room in the shabby yellow rooming house at 2132 Haste Street, except perhaps for an afternoon stroll with the baby down the eucalyptus-shaded paths of the campus. If the Grays should go into San Francisco

for a Saturday-night movie, getting back home well after midnight, baby goes along, too, as he has been doing ever since he was five weeks old and tiny enough to sleep on the seat beside them.

His parents may look thin as a couple of underfed sparrows, but Gary is as fat and saucy as a pampered heir to millions. He has never had a day's sickness, except for a cold, in his life; he is always fed on time and sweetly clean; and he revels in *all* of his mother's attention *all* of the time. There's no other way to manage—not when three of you are living in one room on $109.25 a month.

As far as he knows, Phil Gray is the only student veteran at the University of California who has children, but at least six of the hundred and fifty veterans studying there are married. Most of them are getting a

22.7% of American families have incomes of from $1000 to $2000 a year.

137

How America Lives

THE ONLY PLACE THAT PHIL COULD FIND FOR HIS WIFE AND BABY TO LIVE IN BERKELEY WAS AT AN INCREDIBLE BEEHIVE ROOMING HOUSE, AN OLD-FASHIONED WHITE CLAPBOARD HOUSE THAT FAIRLY SAGGED UNDER THE WEIGHT OF NINETEEN FAMILIES, SIXTEEN OF WHICH WERE YOUNG COUPLES WITH A CHILD EACH. ONE BEDROOM THERE, WITH KITCHEN PRIVILEGES, COST $10 A WEEK PLUS A $2 UTILITY FEE MONTHLY.

College in Ohio anchored a surplus coast guard vessel in the Muskingum River. Four LSTs (landing ships-tanks) were moored in the Hudson River in Troy, New York for veterans attending Rennselaer Polytech Institute.

It was the married housing that most challenged campus leaders and attracted the most press attention. Typically called "Vetsville," the facilities usually consisted of extensive trailer camps and surplus barracks converted to small apartments. Water, lavatories, and showers were shared in central locations. Water for daily use was hauled in buckets. Children played in mud roads and the bitterly cold Wisconsin mornings did not excuse a trip to the community facilities. While many Vetsvilles occupied open spaces on campus, many were miles away.

HOW THE GRAYS SPEND THEIR MONEY

Rent ($25 a month)	$300.00
Utilities	120.00
Food ($10 a week)	520.00
Bank loan	264.00
Payments on furniture	150.00
Clothes	60.00
Baby doctor	40.00
Recreation	50.00
Life insurance ($1000 for Phil, $500 for Gary	67.20
	$1571.20

*From the Ladies Home Journal, an article describing the conditions
and financial situation of a family at the University of California.*

Badger Village in Wisconsin, thirty miles from Madison, developed its own stores, services and elementary school. At the University of Minnesota, veterans housing became known as "Fertile Acres" for good reason.

Many of the colleges and universities which exist today, particularly in the public sector were not established until the late 1950s or 1960s as pressure for higher education grew largely as a result of the example set by veterans. In New York State, then the most populous in the nation, public higher education was scarce and state financial aid was given to private colleges to house students. In 1946 New York established the first "GI college," Champlain College in Plattsburg and soon added others such as at the former Sampson Naval Base.

Most of the more than 3,500 colleges, universities and community colleges in the United States in the 1990s were not in existence until most World War II veterans had left the campuses. The large system known as The State University of New York, for example, with its numerous colleges and universities was not yet established and it was largely in

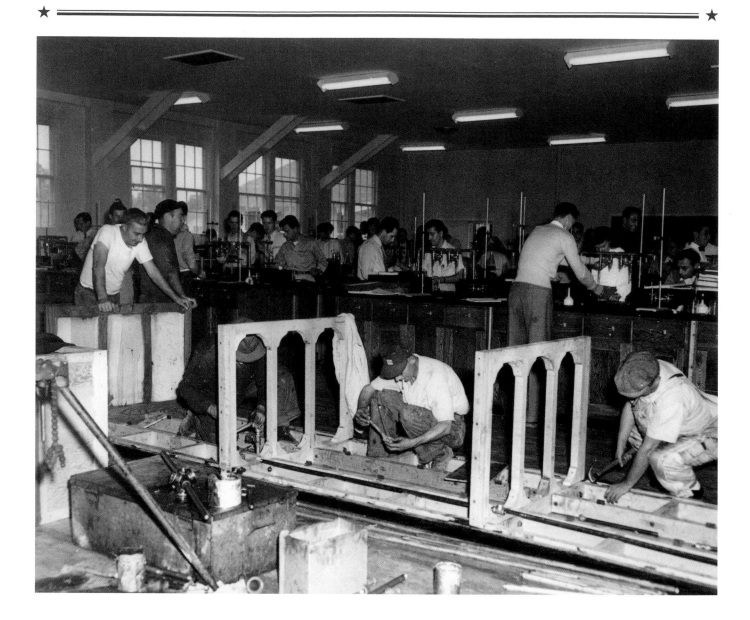

ABOVE: *Students in science lab at the University of Maryland while workmen continue construction.*

LEFT: *Dining at the University of Wisconsin in khakis and flight jackets.*

University of Pittsburgh bookstore.

the 1960s that many small teacher colleges became universities known usually by location, such as Western Michigan University or the University of South Alabama.

Sheer necessity to make higher education responsive to unforeseen and unprecedented demand led to performance of miracles by all involved. At the University of Indiana, for example, a threefold rise in enrollment gave the campus "the general appearance of a vast shipyard in full operation," according to a campus historian. About seventy buildings were under construction in the summer of 1946 and the east side of the campus was pushed back a half mile. A trailer park and small apartment structures went up overnight and army barracks were towed in from various parts of the country. Most of the great state universities shared this experience and few campuses (and few campus towns) escaped the drama of the "energizing" of higher education in America.

Auto repair training in Kansas City, Missouri.

This on-the-job trainee in a doll furniture factory in Jackson, Mississippi, took part in the Normandy Invasion, the Rhine crossing, and the Battle of the Bulge.

Training for a career in advertising in Washington, D.C.

VOCATIONAL EDUCATION

Higher education dominated the scene but education for life and work was in full swing everywhere, spurred on by the same generous provisions of the GI Bill of Rights. Recall that millions of men in service had very little education. The military had done an excellent job of creating techniques for teaching a wide array of subjects from reading to high technology to millions of people of varied backgrounds.

Harry Belafonte, the distinguished singer and actor, tells "I didn't hardly finish first term high school. I had no desire to read, to learn . . . most of the men in my outfit were unskilled black workers, unskilled laborers. And how do you then compete for jobs if you have no training . . . It is in this respect that I think the GI Bill became a God-send." The GI Bill enabled people to reach for the middle class, said Belafonte and "once we had access to education, to knowledge, to skill, we could upgrade ourselves."

Many veterans completed their high school education through the General Educational Development Testing Service of the American Council on Education, an exam still in use, known as the GED. Others, their interests stimulated by military training continued on in vocational training schools in electronics, medical services or business schools. Employers were encouraged to train their own workers with the help of the GI Bill, thereby facilitating movement into the working mainstream. Now-famous movie stars, Tony Curtis, Harry Belafonte, Walter Matthau and Rod Steiger used their GI Bill rights to study

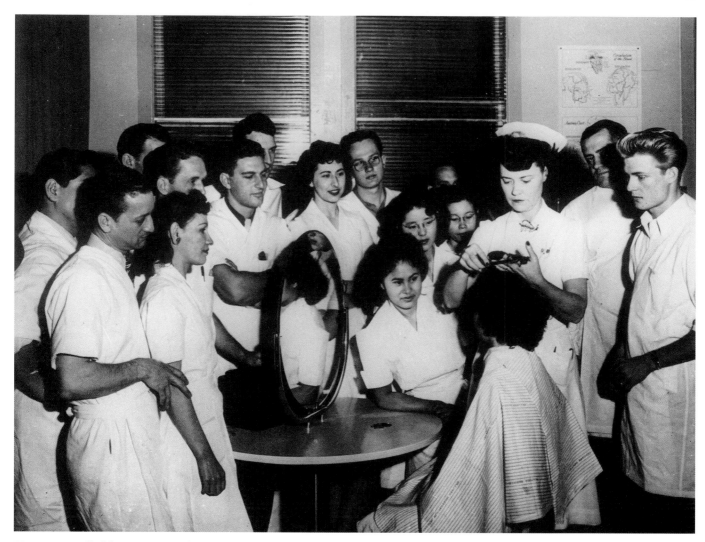

Veterans enrolled for a nine month course of study in a "beauty culture" school in San Francisco. The Veterans Administration paid the tuition plus a monthly stipend to each student.

drama at the New School for Social Research in New York. Still others took training in agriculture and farming, changing the ways of prewar rural life to adapt scientific and technical knowledge to food production and land management.

Among the many lasting legacies of the GI Bill of Rights is the acceptance of continuing lifelong education, of the continuing upgrading of skills and the joining of government, employers and workers in making educational opportunities available. In any post high school educational program today, eighteen-year-olds barely outnumber those over twenty-five.

STANLEY KOSIEROWSKI

"After applying to Fordham University Pharmacy, they told me they had the GI Bill of Rights and I could get my tuition and pay for my books, and that's how I learned about the GI Bill of Rights."

CRADLE OF FREE ENTERPRISE

BY FRANK GERVASI

PHOTOGRAPHS FOR COLLIER'S BY INI VERN—PIX

James Dechaine (left) is one veteran who was able to start his own business—a farm in Minnesota. With him is Farm Agent William Cummins

Ex-Marine Lieutenant Marie Marcelle started a dress shop in East Setauket, L. I., with her own money. She hopes soon to go to a school of fashion designing

ACTUALLY THE NUMBER OF NEW SMALL BUSINESSES DOES NOT EVEN BEGIN TO SERVE AS AN ADEQUATE INDEX OF THE NUMBER OF INDIVIDUALS WHO WANT TO GET INTO BUSINESS FOR THEMSELVES AND CAN'T. TAKE THE RETURNING VETERANS AS AN EXAMPLE. THERE'S A CLAUSE IN THE SO-CALLED GI BILL OF RIGHTS WHICH PROVIDES THAT THE VETERANS' ADMINISTRATION CAN GUARANTEE UP TO 50 PERCENT OF A MAXIMUM OF $4,000 BORROWED FROM A BANK BY A VETERAN FOR AN ADVENTURE INTO A BUSINESS. THE PROVISION STIPULATES THAT THE PROPERTY INVOLVED BE USEFUL AND PRODUCTIVE AND THAT THE VETERAN BE CAPABLE OF OPERATING IT.

From an article in *Collier's*

Seen here in an article from *Collier's*,

FOR YOUNG HIGH SCHOOL GRADUATES OF THE
POST-WAR YEARS, THE GI BILL PRESENTED A
PROBLEM. JOBS WENT TO RETURNING VETERANS;
THE YOUNG GRADUATE WAS STILL APT TO BE
DRAFTED. EMPLOYERS PREFERRED VETERANS
TOO BECAUSE UNCLE SAM FOOTED ON-THE-JOB
TRAINING. OFTEN, APPLICATIONS TO COLLEGE
WERE DENIED WITH "DUE TO THE GREAT
NUMBER OF APPLICATIONS FROM VETERANS."

ABOVE: *On-the-job training on furniture.*

LEFT: *An on-the-job trainee in oil heating installation. The veteran trainee received the GI subsistence allowance in addition to an apprentice wage paid by the company.*

BELOW: *Former GIs on a Cherokee Reservation in North Carolina, learning a trade under a GI Bill training program.*

EMPLOYERS WERE ENCOURAGED TO TRAIN THEIR OWN WORKERS WITH THE HELP OF THE GI BILL.

DR. ARNOLD LEAR

His work with the wounded while serving in the transport service in the Atlantic reinforced his desire to go to medical school.

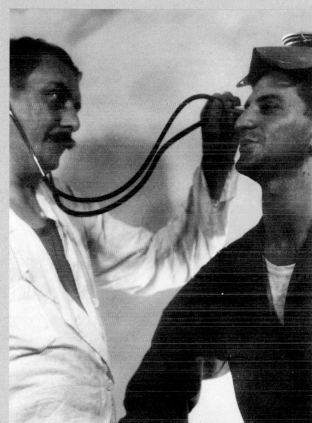

ABOVE: *A bit of horseplay while traveling aboard a Liberty ship ferrying troops to Europe.*

RIGHT: *American, British, and Canadian Army and Navy servicemen and women at a USO function in London. Dr. Lear is seated fourth from left.*

ANDREW BRIMMER

"The black schools that really benefited disproportionately were the small black liberal arts colleges, unrelated to the state-many of them church related. Now they could compete for students who could come, not needing scholarships from the institution, bringing their GI Bill benefits. They had their own funds for stipend, they got tuitions paid, and the institutions got some grants.

Now while we've concentrated on the benefits to college students, we must remind ourselves that most of the students who got benefits under the GI Bill did not go to colleges and universities. They went to specialized training schools and so on. And so many of the black institutions that wouldn't qualify as colleges and universities were able to offer training-where the training qualified, although not strictly in academics. So many blacks got skills through these kinds of programs. So the benefits of the GI Bill were pervasive."

LEFT: *Andrew Brimmer noted economist and former member of the Federal Reserve Board.*

Farm training was available under the GI Bill. Shown here is a veteran in training before buying his own farm on a VA loan.

BELOW: *GI training program at a watchmaking school in Cleveland, Ohio.*

WILLIS MESSIAH

"I served four years in the Army and studied architecture at Catholic University on the GI Bill. I had a forty-year career in architecture. The GI Bill was a generous reward which many did not take advantage of. It was there for veterans, you just had to take advantage of it, but the key was that it *was* available."

Willis Messiah with fellow servicemen.

RIGHT: *Messiah appears second from left.*

BELOW: *Back row center.*

22

A home in the street. Many Los Angeles families, evicted from houses and apartments, have no other place to go

CHAOS ON THE COAST

BY JIM MARSHALL

The SRO signs are out in California, relief costs go soaring—and still the sun-hungry hordes are rolling in

WHEN the war quit the West Coast leaned back and had a dream. Now all the two million workers who had flooded in from the Middle West and South would hit the trail east over US 66 and 10 and 20 and 30 and 50. The millions of soldiers who had crammed into camps, the scores of thousands of sailors and Marines who had jammed every port from Seattle to San Diego, would scatter. The wives and families who had followed their fighting men to the Coast would go back home. Airplane factories, shipyards, lumber mills, munitions plants would either close down or get "back to normal."

Now maybe someone would be able to get a room in a hotel, or see a movie without standing in line for an hour, or eat in a restaurant without lining up and bribing the headwaiter, or roll the highways Sundays with a few feet between bumpers. Nothing like this happened.

The Coast today has more people than it had during the war years; the trend of travel, instead of being east, is still west. States like Oklahoma, Louisiana, the Carolinas, Montana, the Dakotas, Georgia, which lost population—up to 300,000 a state in some cases—still haven't got back their missing people.

The out-of-staters, instead of going home, have sent East for friends and families; so have fighting men who, after stopping briefly on the Coast on their way to the Pacific, could hardly wait to get back and settle down between the Rockies and the Sierras and the ocean.

As fall approached, another influx of new settlers got ready to move into southern California. These were the shipyard and plane-factory workers who emigrated from the Middle West and South to the North Pacific Coast during the war. Since the victory, they had been living on savings, on War Bonds, on unemployment doles in the Puget Sound and Columbia River country. Now, the money was about gone and what to do?

"Why, southern California, of course," they said, as the rains set in and no jobs turned up in lumbering or fishing or farm work. "You can live in California for next to nothing; don't need any heat; pick oranges anywhere . . ."

It is curious how that old myth lives on—despite the fact that living costs in California are far above the national average, that you *do* need heat, and that a good way to get in jail for six months is to rob an orange grove.

As the rains started in the Pacific Northwest, the old cars loaded with families and family belongings sputtered south down US 101 and US 99 and from central Washington and Oregon, down US 97. They were headed for the sunny Southland, and how they would live, or where, they didn't seem to know.

Neither did the sunny Southland.

Meanwhile, people who had a little dough tried to build homes. . . .

Twenty-three miles from Los Angeles City Hall we sat with Bill Ivins, a combat veteran, inside the stark studding of a home he had been trying to build since February.

"Look," he said, "you may not believe it, but I had to get exactly one hundred and two permits, licenses and priorities before I started to build. Count 'em!" He dug wads of them out of a battered brief case.

"This place—if I ever get it finished, which I begin to doubt—will set me back about $17,000," he said. "The builders tell me ten months is normal time for building a six-room home today. My place here is built on the same plans my old man used out in Westwood in 1931. It cost him $6,500 and it took seven weeks to build—out of good seasoned Douglas fir.

"Look at this stuff!" he ran a hand along a skinny, unseasoned two-by-four. "What's going to happen to the stucco when this dries out?"

All over southern California are thousands of these home skeletons, ten, twenty, thirty-five per cent completed—and temporarily abandoned for lack of labor and material—more than a year after the last shot was fired.

In August the National Association of Home Builders said that in southern California only seven per cent of the new homes started since January had been completed. Ninety-three out of every hundred still were uninhabitable.

By mid-1946 California—especially southern California — was acquiring puzzle wrinkles, and not just about buildings, either. More than a million dollars

(Continued on page 59)

Hundreds of Californians are living in old streetcars. Here a fair client gets a sales demonstration

PHOTOGRAPHS FOR COLLIER'S BY JACK MANNING-PIX

THE LOAN PROGRAM

A FAMILY AND HOME OF YOUR OWN

The home loan provisions of the GI Bill were arguably more important than the educational opportunities in changing America. The Great Depression and the short supply of building materials during four years of war led to a severe nationwide housing shortage. This condition was exacerbated by the urbanization of the nation and the increase in industrial concentration in major cities. In California, for example, which was a center for new war industries, such as aircraft production, the population grew by two million but the number of homes remained stagnant.

Across the nation, millions of returning veterans and their families doubled up. Like the college campuses, cities and towns filled with trailer camps and military style barracks. Families set up homemaking in rooming houses, garages and attics.

A February, 1946 article in *Collier's,* "No Place To Live," called the housing shortage "a national problem as serious and compelling as war itself." It was not just the lack of new housing that resulted from more than fifteen years of depression and war, but existing homes had fallen into disrepair and entire neighborhoods deteriorated. Even as some building resumed, materials from nails to shingles were in short supply. Homebuilders had to compete with those building the stores and office buildings needed to restart the economy. It was not unusual for people with housing to rent to demand extra funds "under the table" or to charge exorbitant prices for shoddy furnishings. *Fortune* magazine reported in April 1946 that after a man was arrested in Norwood, Ohio for strangling his wife, five telephone calls were received from people who wanted to buy his house.

Estimates called for the need for about six million new housing units. Twice that many needed repair or total replacement. By early 1946, 1.5 million veterans were living doubled up with family or friends. Discharged GIs, marrying in record setting numbers with no place to live posed serious personal and social dangers common in overcrowded conditions. President Harry S. Truman named former Louisville, Kentucky mayor Wilson Wyatt as housing expediter with power to cut through red tape to establish priorities for production and allocation of housing materials.

Prior to entering military service, returning veterans had barely begun the normal life processes of jobs, marriage, children, and house-

OPPOSITE AND PP 74, 75, AND 76: *As millions of veterans returned home, the pressure for housing of any sort assumed alarming proportions all over the country, as seen in these articles from* Collier's.

holds. In 1946 alone, the marriage rate in the United States increased by fifty percent over the 1944 rate, with 2.3 million marriages followed by an enormous boom in the birth rate. Women who had worked in civilian and defense industries returned to traditional roles of managing households and caring for children. In 1996 and 1997, an extraordinary number of golden (fifty year) wedding anniversaries were celebrated

The loan guarantee program enabled millions of Americans to realize the American Dream by transforming the majority from renters to homeowners.

One purpose of the loan program was to place veterans on a par with civilians who had time to develop traditional credit ratings. The ensuing building boom released the energies of the entire economy from banking to all forms of consumer goods.

The initial loan program provided for a VA guarantee of up to fifty percent of the loan amount at four percent interest. While the details varied with a changing economy, Congress has maintained generous provisions for veterans housing needs up to the present day.

More than two million loans

> Miami Beach just prior to and following Pearl Harbor. Residents watched in horror as U-Boats torpedoed United Nations boats less than three miles off shore. . . . As AAF officers and men returned . . . the OPA actually had to force one landlady to permit a young sergeant to bring his wife and newborn baby home to his own apartment from the hospital.

were arranged by 1950 and more than five million by the end of that decade. Millions of families moved to a place called "the suburbs" and gave new shape to family life in America.

The most famous of these new suburbs was Levittown, former farmland on Long Island, New York, just thirty miles east of Manhattan. William Levitt who had served in the Navy as a "seabee," (for *construction battalion*, "CB") adapted assembly line techniques, putting houses on the market at the rate of thirty-five-a-day and sold them for about $7,500. By 1960 more than 65,000 people lived there, almost a third of them under the age of ten. Similar developments emerged everywhere.

Little wonder that veteran Karl Heymann recalls with laughter how he bought his house: "I called the builder up and said I'll buy one and he said don't you want to look at it and I said no." Veteran Jerry Naples tells of his visit to Levittown. His wife told him that if he had a choice, to get a yellow kitchen. "What she didn't know, and I didn't know either, they were all yellow."

Levittown's magic is recalled by veteran George Merritt who still lives there. "No money down. I can afford that. And I get four rooms,

> MILLIONS OF FAMILIES
> MOVED TO A PLACE CALLED
> "THE SUBURBS" AND GAVE
> NEW SHAPE TO FAMILY LIFE
> IN AMERICA.

GEORGE MERRITT

"Bill Levitt died so I called up the commander and I said look, I know how to work it out so that we can go to the funeral and we'll go there with the color guard. And he said okay, if you can work it out. We honored him by being there with the American flag and the American Legion flag."

"I moved into Levittown when I was twenty-seven years old, and I'm there forty-two years. The basic house was the same plan, the basic house. On the outside, they looked a little bit different. I mean, you could tell one from the other. One had a dropped roof. The other had two doors. Another model had a jalousie window. So they were a little bit different, but the basic house inside was exactly the same-the kitchen, the living room, the dining room in the Cape Cods were all exactly the same."

George Merritt still lives in Levittown.

VA loans changed the topography of America.

and there's a washing machine. . . . Oh, it was unbelievable." Settlement charges amounted to about $300, mortgages were for forty years at less than $75 per month.

For some time the 60 × 100 foot plots were governed by strict rules on lawns, shrubs, hanging laundry, paint colors, all designed to maintain a middle class life style. Until a shopping center was built, salesmen in vans circled the streets with groceries and staples. Today, almost every house has been remodeled but one recent purchaser of a home there told *The Washington Post* in a story of the fiftieth anniversary of Levittown that it is a "piece of America. A place for an average guy, a nobody, to have a chance." Levittown in some ways calls forth the images of immigrants coming to America seeking entry to a decent life.

The VA Loan meant that the government co-signed a large part of a veteran's mortgage. This encouraged developers, under governmental supervision to build, bankers to lend and veterans to buy. The resulting explosion in consumer demand stirred the entrepreneurial spirit of American manufacturers. The VA loan literally changed the topography and social structure of America.

The impact was enormous. Communities of young families, schools,

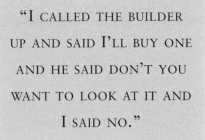

Levittown 1947. A house in the suburbs, new friends, and a community to build.

Open house—post World War II housing search.

cars, roads, shopping centers, and churches dotted the landscape. Instead of crowding the existing great cities, veterans laid claim to the vacant countryside. World War II veterans played a major role in building communities, developing public services, and in meeting civic responsibilities. They had a stake in the nation.

ART BUCHWALD

I think the GI Bill was one of the greatest things America did, as well as the Marshall Plan. It created a generation of people that were hard working, that cared, and could appreciate education after having been through the war. I just think enough credit had not been given to what they did for these kids.

I think what the country did was invest in it's GIs and it paid off. I resent the fact that it's been called some sort of welfare program when in fact, it was an investment.

I have found out in America over the years, if something works, it doesn't get any publicity. If it's a disaster, you hear about it all the time.

The American Dream home.

With a GI business loan this veteran went into a young and growing business, manufacturing precision gears.

BUSINESS AND FARM LOANS

Just as the vocational and job training portions of the GI Bill lacked the glamour of veterans at colleges and universities, so too did the business and farm loans aspects of the bill get lost in the shadows of home ownership. The bulk of farm and business loans were made right after demobilization at the rate of more than 2,000 farm loans and more than 4,000 business loans monthly. Most of the loans went for equipment, machinery, fixtures, livestock and working capital. By the end of 1947, the VA guaranteed 1.1 million home loans, 100,000 business loans and 40,000 farm loans.

The loans were small but enough to encourage a start-up business or to join in partnership with others. Three brothers in St. Paul,

Pharmacist started his own drug store with VA loan.

Minnesota, all veterans, started a successful road surfacing business. Former Women's Army Corps (WAC) Dorothy D. Chamberlain, bought a farm with the aid of a GI loan. Most veterans preferred either to continue their education or find a place in the burgeoning manufacturing and service corporations which characterized post World War II America.

JUDGE
WILLIAM NORRIS

"The GI Bill was definitely, in my mind, the ticket for all of us who were fortunate to have received those benefits. For all of us, the GI Bill was the ticket to the realization of the American Dream, defined in terms of a good education, a home that we own, a family with enough resources to make sure our children got a decent education, and a satisfying career in the sense of the feeling of fulfillment that we all thrive when we feel that our own God-given talents are being fully utilized."

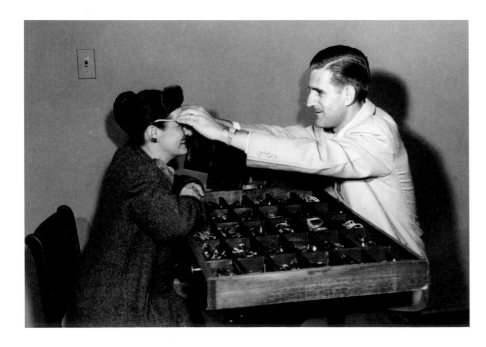

ABOVE: *Three brothers, all veterans, obtained a GI loan to go into the road surfacing business in St. Paul, Minnesota.*

LEFT: *Former marine learned optometry under the GI Bill.*

Woman veteran used a GI business loan to form a partnership with her father in a "junk shop" in Menlo Park, California.

ABOVE: *Army veteran used a GI loan to open his own beauty shop.*

LEFT: *A loan under the GI Bill enabled this Navy veteran to leave his presser job to open his own shop.*

PP 94, 95: *A former WAC on the farm she bought with a VA loan.*

DON BALFOUR

"I was a student at George Washington University at the time, and was the elected, or appointed editor of the school newspaper. The summer school newspaper edition needed a story and it seemed to me that the biggest story going on for college students was the GI Bill. So I called the Veterans Administration and asked to speak to whoever it was that was going to administer the law as soon as it was passed, and got an interview with him.

Went on up to see him and figured I might as well take my discharge with me so

"That was the best time of my life." Balfour was the first veteran to apply for educational benefits.

that when I left the interview, I could leave it with his secretary and ask her to process it whenever the time came. Well, while I was there in the middle of the interview, he got the call from the white house saying that the Bill had been passed. And when the interview was over,, I asked him whether or not I could apply for GI Bill privileges. He said certainly and he called his secretary in.

He dictated a letter from me to him applying for the GI Bill, and that's how I became the first, it was that easy."

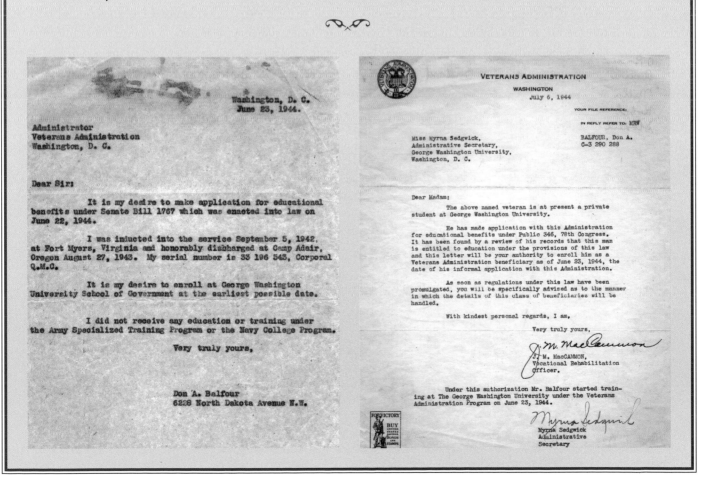

THE INVISIBLE VETERANS

Two classes of veterans were unheralded but significant beneficiaries of the GI Bill: women and black veterans.

Approximately 350,000 women served in the armed forces and were eligible for all GI Bill rights. No records were kept on women's use of various parts of the GI Bill by the VA because their numbers were considered too small. The expectations of the women veterans and the general public was that women had served for patriotic reasons and could be expected to become wives and mothers. Many of the women were unaware of their eligibility or made no claim to it even if they went to school. A few provisions of the GI Bill were discriminatory against women. For example, a married woman veteran could not claim her husband as a dependent and her income did not count in calculations for a GI loan. A widow could receive her husband's benefits but not a widower. Since 1972, women veterans have the same rights as male veterans.

THIS POSTER CONTRIBUTED TO THE WAC BY WAMSUTTA MILLS, NEW BEDFORD, MASS.

During the war, women were vital in maintaining both civilian and military production and services. Women served in all branches of the armed forces, carrying such names as WACs, WAVES, and SPARS. A number of women who were not given military status until many years later ferried planes for the Army Air Force and were known as WASPs—Women's Air Force Service Pilots. A 1985 Harris Survey of women veterans showed that more than half used some portion of the GI Bill but many were not aware that they had been eligible. Many, of course, married and had children.

Kay O'Grady remembers hearing about the chance to join the service and "my first thought was, oh boy, this is my ticket out of Wisconsin." She decided to go to fashion art school "and the GI Bill was my one chance of doing this." Without that training, she said she would "have ended up as a seamstress in a factory" instead of a satisfying career in the fashion industry. "I dread to even think about it," says veteran Kay O'Grady.

Contrary to popular belief, the women's "liberation" movement did not have its origins in the post war period. Most women of that generation became homemakers and mothers, subordinate in many ways

OPPOSITE:
Bulova watchmaking training shop.

The veteran's club University of Maryland.

to the ambitions of the sixteen million men who served in the armed forces. Preference in jobs and college admissions went to males. It would be the daughters of that post war generation who sought to emulate the success of their fathers.

❧

The GI experience for black Americans was mixed but reflective of America's racial dilemma. World War II was fought under a system of legal racial segregation. In 1940 nearly eighty percent of the black population lived in the seventeen segregationist southern states and the District of Columbia. Most black Americans who went to college before the war went to historically black colleges and universities and only 1.2 percent of college graduates were black. Though blacks constituted sizeable portions of the population in those southern states, there might be one black college for every nine or ten white colleges and no graduate or professional programs for blacks.

After the war, the black colleges were inundated by veteran students. Their enrollments increased by fifty percent and many veterans were turned away or assisted by states to attend schools elsewhere. One beneficial result was increased federal support for buildings and equipment at the historically black institutions. Black college enrollment increased from a prewar 1.08 percent to 3.6 percent in 1950.

OVERLEAF: *Thousands of black veterans attended all-black Universities in the segregated South. Wayne State University in Detroit, Michigan estimated that nearly a third of the veterans enrolled there were black.*

KAY O'GRADY

"I first heard about the GI Bill when I was being mustered out. They were talking about the advantage of being discharged, because so many of the people were unhappy to be leaving, but at the end of the war, all the women were being discharged so I didn't know if they just thought it would soften the blow or what. But then I realized that the GI Bill was legitimate, that you could actually go to college and have your tuition and books paid for. Even the fact that you got some extra money didn't seem to make much of an imprint. But the fact that you got your tuition and books which is a big item. So that was my plan to use that. Without the GI Bill I couldn't have possibly had a college degree."

Cherokee Indian veteran receiving instruction in radio repair with the assistance of the VA job training program.

These figures do not include the thousands of black veterans who attended northern and western colleges for which no accurate numbers exist. Wayne State University in Detroit, Michigan, for example, estimates that nearly a third of the veterans enrolled there during 1946–1950 were black.

Black veterans could take advantage of VA loans but discrimination kept the loan program from making a major impact on the black community. In retrospect historically regrettable, black veterans were prohibited from buying in Levittown and in similar communities. Very few black families live in Levittown to this day. The contribution that the VA loan program could have made to racially integrated housing was never realized and has dramatically affected American society. Nevertheless, the GI Bill had an enormous impact upon the marginalized black population. It is responsible in substantial measure for today's

DOVEY ROUNDTREE

When young WAC Captain Dovey Johnson was barred from a Miami bus late one night in 1943 and forced to yield her place to a white soldier standing behind her, she was, she remembers, "absolutely defenseless." For a black person riding buses in the Deep South—even one traveling on official Army business, as Roundtree was then—there was no escaping the long arm of racial segregation laws.

Just a few years later, the government that had segregated its armed services and made separate-but-equal a part of American life, gave Roundtree the means to undo those wrongs. It was the GI Bill that opened the door to law school for the 31-year-old veteran, thus catapulting her into the thick of the civil rights movement. As a Howard University Law student, Roundtree found herself at the center of the group of black attorneys leading the charge against segregation.

Inspired by such giants as James M. Nabritt and George E. C. Hayes, Roundtree, as a newly-admitted member of the D.C. Bar, took on the case of a young black woman named Sarah Keys, a WAC ousted from a segregated North Carolina bus just as Roundtree herself had been in Florida a decade earlier. The three year legal battle that ensued culminated in the 1955 landmark decision of the Interstate Commerce Commission banning segregation in interstate bus travel. Dovey Roundtree went on to a distinguished career in civil and criminal law, setting legal precedent with a number of other cases and becoming mentor to dozens of young black attorneys. She sees her journey from life in the segregationist South to the halls of federal courthouses as testament to the infinite possibility of a government which, though imperfect, provides its citizens the means for change. In her case, the GI Bill allowed her to take the first giant step forward, providing the means for her to go to law school.

"Democracy," she says, is not a fixed thing. It is always becoming. And it falls to each of us to do for America what the hymn says so beautifully: 'to mend thine every flaw.' In doing that, we help it to become all that it can be."

TOP: *WAC Captain Dovey Johnson, recruiting for the WAC, October 1942*

MIDDLE LEFT: *Dovey Roundtree on the steps of the U.S. District Court.*

MIDDLE RIGHT: *Graduation from Howard University Law School, 1950*

BOTTOM LEFT: *Sarah Louise Keys, WAC.*

black middle class of professionals and business leaders. Noted economist and former member of the Federal Reserve Board Andrew Brimmer, whose father was a farm laborer, tells how as a result of the GI Bill he earned a Ph.D. degree at Harvard, an event he treasures more "than the day Lyndon Johnson appointed me to the Federal Reserve." Harry Belafonte speaks for all GIs when he says that had it not been for the GI Bill "I'm not quite sure what I'd have been."

Since World War II, a high percentage of the armed forces are women and minorities and these servicemen and women have been encouraged to participate in contemporary versions of the GI Bill.

"WHAT THE GI BILL DID WAS IT GAVE US THE QUALIFICATIONS OR THE CREDENTIALS TO COMPETE FOR JOBS THAT WOULD ULTIMATELY LEAD US INTO THE MIDDLE CLASS. . . . ONCE WE HAD ACCESS TO EDUCATION, TO KNOWLEDGE, TO SKILL WE COULD UPGRADE OURSELVES"

Harry Belafonte

"WELL, IT'S INTERESTING. WOMEN WHO HAVE ALWAYS BEEN THE SUPPORT OF THEIR CHILDREN, THEIR HUSBANDS AND THEIR FAMILIES, I THINK, HAVE AN IDENTITY AS HAVING A SUPPORTIVE ROLE. AND MANY OF THE WOMEN THAT I SPOKE TO WHEN I WAS WRITING THE BOOK I WROTE ON WOMEN VETERANS BACK IN THE 80S, AND INTERVIEWING WORLD WAR II WOMEN, MANY WOMEN SURPRISINGLY THOUGHT OF THEMSELVES IN SUPPORTIVE ROLES, THAT THAT'S WHAT WOMEN SHOULD DO. THEIR ROLES ARE SUPPORTIVE AND THE COUNTRY NEEDED THEM, SO THEY WERE SUPPORTIVE. AND BELIEVE IT OR NOT, MANY OF THEM AFTER THE WAR, DID NOT THINK OF THEMSELVES AS VETERANS. AND WE KNOW THAT BECAUSE SOME OF THEM SAID THEY DIDN'T KNOW THEY WERE ELIGIBLE FOR VETERANS BENEFITS. AN ASTONISHING THING BECAUSE ON THE WHOLE, THE VETERANS BENEFITS SYSTEM, UNDER THE GI BILL, WAS PRETTY EQUAL."

June Willenz

THE GI BILL LIVES ON

The GI Bill established the basic structure for rewarding military service. Veterans of the Korean and Vietnam conflicts received similar though somewhat less generous educational benefits and significant home loan guarantees. The first peacetime GI Bill had its inception after the draft officially ended on December 31, 1972 and an All Volunteer Force (AVP) was put in place. As recruitment proved difficult, particularly after the Vietnam experience, the Veterans Educational Assistance Program (VEAP) was enacted, effective December, 1976. Continuing problems with recruitment in numbers and quality led in 1981 to efforts to enact a "New GI Bill" and a temporary program began in 1984. In 1987, President Ronald Reagan signed a law

President Reagan signs newest GI Bill renaming it "Montgomery GI Bill." Montgomery is standing to the left of President Reagan.

designating it as permanent and renamed it the "Montgomery GI Bill" (MGIB) in honor of Representative G. V. "Sonny" Montgomery of Mississippi who had led the effort for many years.

Montgomery served in the military during World War II and the Korean War and for many years served as chairman of the House Committee on Veterans' Affairs. Writing on behalf of the American Council on Education's observance of the 50th anniversary of the GI Bill, Congressman Montgomery noted:

> "With the stroke of his pen, President Roosevelt transformed the face and future of American Society. Higher education, which had been the privilege of the fortunate few, became part of the American dream—available to all citizens who served their country through military service. No longer were the hopes and expectations of young Americans of modest economic means restricted because the key to advancement—higher education—was beyond their reach. Few, if any, more important pieces of legislation have been enacted by Congress, and no government investment has paid richer dividends to us all."

Art Buchwald summed it up for all beneficiaries of the GI Bill of Rights. "I'm glad to say thank you to somebody because it was good and it helped me very much, and there are some things that hurt some people and help others. I'm under the impression that it didn't hurt anybody. I don't know where I would have been without the GI Bill."

Montgomery (left) *in uniform.*

REFLECTIONS ON A DREAM

The meaning and value of the GI Bill of Rights is not subject to measurement despite the availability of numbers and statistics. It is a classic case of the idea that "the things that count cannot be counted." The GI Bill set the country upon a course which, prior to the attack on Pearl Harbor on December 7, 1941, no one could have foreseen. The fears that prewar experiences generated about what the future might bring and which gave birth to the GI Bill were met and conquered: unemployment, unrest, social dissatisfaction, and even potential revolution.

No one could or did forecast the positive and durable impact The GI Bill of Rights would have upon the social fabric of the nation. Notable among these lasting legacies are:

- It was a law that worked. It ranks among the most important laws ever passed in the nation's history and one of the very few that has no known responsible critics. It is still looked upon with appreciation, reverence, and respect.

- The GI Bill was rooted in the idea that the individual recipient of a benefit, not the government, could decide how and where to use it. This challenged existing cultural and institutional barriers and made possible the American ideal of individual opportunity for upward mobility.

- It established education—the knowledge society—as the hallmark of freedom and achievement, available to anyone regardless of origin, regardless of age, regardless of race or religion, and regardless of marital or family status.

- It turned the nation into one of stakeholders—"independent yeoman" in Thomas Jefferson's phrase—self-confident and self-respecting owners of homes and businesses, not beholden to social superiors, ready to take responsibility for their families and communities.

- It made possible a quick restoration of the nation's human, economic, and social capital which had been restrained or distorted by the Great Depression and the Great War, thereby catapulting the United States to leadership on the world stage.

- The success of the GI Bill of 1944 led to continued usage of its major themes for all veterans of subsequent American wars. It now serves as an inducement for enlistment in America's volunteer military forces. The GI Bill lives on.

THE EVOLVING GI BILL

World War II GI Bill

Veterans were eligible for education benefits under the Servicemen's Readjustment Act of 1944 if they served during World War II for at least 90 days and received other than a dishonorable discharge. Veterans were entitled to a maximum of 48 months of training, depending upon their length of service. The Veterans Administration (VA) paid the schools a maximum of $500 a year for tuition and other costs and paid single veterans a living allowance of $50 a month; married veterans received $65 a month. Of a veterans' population of 15.4 million, some 7.8 million, or 50.5 percent, received education or training under the bill- 2.2 million of them at colleges and universities.

Home loan guaranties boomed during the same period. From June 22, 1944, until passage of the Korean GI Bill, VA backed 2,360,603 home loans. In 1947, the peak year for World War II veterans, VA approved 640,298 loans, including 562,985 for homes, 24,690 for farms and 52,623 for businesses.

Korean Conflict GI Bill

Veterans were eligible for education assistance under the Veterans' Readjustment Assistance Act of 1952 if they served 90 days after June 27, 1950, and received other than a dishonorable discharge. The VA paid the veterans up to $110 a month out of which the veteran paid for tuition, books, fees, supplies and other training costs and living expenses for up to 36 months.

Of a veterans' population of approximately 5.5 million, nearly 2.4 million were trained, including 1.2 million at colleges and universities.

During the Korean War period, June 27, 1950, through Jan. 31, 1955, VA approved 1,553,367 home loans for veterans.

Post-Korean and Vietnam Era GI Bill

The Veterans Readjustment Benefits Act of 1966 provided education assistance to those who served in the post-Korean conflict era and the Vietnam era. The program became effective June 1, 1966, and was available to veterans who served after January 31, 1955. Veterans were eligible if they had served more than 180 days

and had received other than a dishonorable discharge. For the first time, active duty personnel were eligible for the benefits, which began at up to $100 a month and increased to $311 a month by 1977.

Of the post-Korean conflict veterans' population of 3 million, 1.4 million received training, including nearly three-quarters of a million at colleges and universities. Of the Vietnam era veterans' population of 10.3 million, 6.8 million received education or training under the bill, including 4.3 million at colleges and universities.

During the Post-Korean–Vietnam Era period of 1955-1975, more than 4,500,000 home loans were guaranteed by VA.

Veterans Educational Assistance Program (VEAP)

VEAP was enacted as an incentive to enlist in the armed services between December 1976 and March 31, 1987. To be eligible, service members were required to serve more than 180 days, receive other than a dishonorable discharge, and contribute to the plan. The VA matched contributions at the rate of $2 for every $1 contributed by participants, who contributed from $25 to $100 a month for a maximum of $2,700. Benefits were paid monthly for up to 36 months. Participants who dropped out of the program had their contributions refunded. Service members had ten years from the date of last discharge or release from active duty to claim VEAP benefits. The VA extended the ten-year period if the individual could not train because of a disability or because of being held by a foreign government or power.

More than 668,000 veterans received education and training benefits under VEAP.

Montgomery GI Bill-Active Duty (MGIB)

MGIB was created for volunteers who began active military duty after July 1, 1985. Public Law 100-48 allows participants to have their pay reduced by $100 a month for their first 12 months on active duty. In exchange, the VA pays them up to $400 a month for 36 months of college or other training. Eligible individuals include those who served the initial active duty commitment and receive an honorable discharge. Individuals must decide whether to participate when they begin active duty, and decisions not to participate are irrevocable. The military pay reduction is not refundable. Eligibility for MGIB benefits expires ten years from the date of the veterans' discharge. The VA can extend this period if the individual was prevented from training because of a disability or because he or she was held by a foreign government or power.

Montgomery GI Bill-Selected Reserve

The Selected Reserve GI Bill expands education benefits to reservists. Participants are members of military Selected Reserves of the Army or Air National Guard. To be eligible, reservists must enlist, reenlist, or extend their enlistments after June 30, 1985, for a six year period, complete the Initial Active Duty for Training, and remain in good standing in their reserve units. Unlike the active duty program, there is no pay reduction. Eligible participants receive monthly payments, which were raised to a maximum of $190 a month after April 1, 1993, and which are adjusted annually for cost-of-living increases.

Survivors' and Dependents' Educational Assistance

This program provides education assistance for dependents of veterans whose service-connected disabilities are permanent and total and for survivors of veterans who died from service-connected causes. Spouses and children of service personnel who are missing in action or who are interred by a hostile foreign government for more than 90 days also are eligible. Individuals may receive up to $404 a month for up to 45 months of education or training at approved institutions.

Vocational Rehabilitation

Initiated after World War I, this program provides veterans who have service-related disabilities with education and vocational training benefits. Veterans may receive training for four or more years and may receive subsistence allowances in addition to their disability compensation. Eligible veterans may enroll at schools or colleges or in on-the-job training programs or apprenticeship programs, pursue institutional on-farm training, enter other programs that combine school and job training, or train at special rehabilitation facilities or at home (if severe disabilities preclude training at outside facilities).

The Loan Guarantee Program

When the loan guaranty program began in 1944, the maximum amount of guaranty was limited to 50 percent of the loan for a maximum of $2,000. Loans were limited to a maximum of 20 years and a maximum interest rate of 4 percent. To be eligible, a veteran must have served in the active U.S. military forces for a period of 90 days or more any time on or after September 16, 1940, and before official termination of World War II. Changes in the program were enacted in 1945. The maximum amount of guaranty available was increased to $4,000. The maximum maturity for real estate loans was extended to 25 years and for farms loans to 40 years.

Congress in 1950 increased the maximum guaranty to 60 percent of the loan amount, not to exceed $7,500, and lengthened the maximum maturity of loans from 25 to 30 years. More significantly, the program was opened to unremarried widows of veterans who had died in service or as a result of service-connected injury or disease. The Korean GI Bill in 1952 extended home loan guaranties to Korean War veterans.

In 1966, the Veterans' Readjustment Benefits Act made post-Korean veterans eligible for home loan guaranties and direct loans. The law for the first time also expanded the program to include active-duty personnel who had served at least two years. The law also authorized the VA to adjust the VA home loan interest rate ceiling according to the demands of the loan market.

The Veterans' Housing Act in 1970 removed limiting dates on using the benefit. By eliminating the expiration dates for entitlement, benefits were restored to 9 million World War II and Korean Conflict veterans.

Numerous refinements and extensions of the home loan provisions have been made to include veterans of other wars including the Persian Gulf war, peacetime veterans, men and women on active duty, surviving spouses and reservists. Nearly 15 million loans have enabled those who served the nation in uniform become homeowners.

Index

Photo Credits

Every attempt has been made to identify individual photographs for proper credit.

American Council on Education: 40, 42–43, 48,49 (center, bottom), 53 (top), 59, 98

American Legion: 13, 14, 15, 16, 17 (top right)

Don Balfour: 93

Andrew Brimmer: 68

Art Buchwald: 83

Senator Bob Dole: 7

Harvard University: 42–43

Indiana University: 35, 37, 50, 51, 53 (center)

Stanley Kosierowski: 63

Ladies Home Journal: 56, 57

Dr. Arnold Lear: 67

Leon Lederman: 41

Marietta College: 52

George Merritt: 77

Willis Messiah: 71

Joan Munkacsi: 56, 57

Dr. Jerry Naples: 55

National Archives: 2, 6, 9, 13 (bottom right), 20, 25, 28–29, 36, 45, 49 (top), 58, 66 (bottom), 78, 79, 80–81, 82, 84, 85

Judge William Norris: 89

Kay O'Grady: 99

Dovey Roundtree: 103

State Historical Society of Wisconsin: 44

University of Denver: 38–39

University of Maryland: 49 (center, bottom), 53 (bottom), 56 (top), 58 (top), 98

University of Wisconsin: 40, 46–47, 49, 58 (bottom)

Veterans Administration: 60, 61, 62, 66 (top, center), 68 (top), 69, 70, 78, 87, 88, 90, 91, 92, 94–95, 96, 102

Wayne State University, Archives of Labor and Urban Affairs: 34, 100–101